The Buzz on Honeybees

By Cathy Kaemmerlen

Illustrated by Kathy Coates

PELICAN PUBLISHING COMPANY

Gretna 2012

To Jim Ovbey and Cindy Bee.
Many thanks for your help with the buzz.

The word "Pelican" and the depiction of a pelican are
trademarks of Pelican Publishing Company, Inc., and are
registered in the U.S. Patent and Trademark Office.

ISBN 9781455614578

Printed in Singapore

Published by Pelican Publishing Company, Inc.
1000 Burmaster Street, Gretna, Louisiana 70053

THE BUZZ ON HONEYBEES

I am Itty Bitty Betty, the Storytelling Honeybee. Instead of just collecting nectar like the other honeybees, I buzz around collecting stories. There "bee" a lot of stories to tell, and my ears are buzzing.

Itty Bitty Betty—she's a honey of a bee!

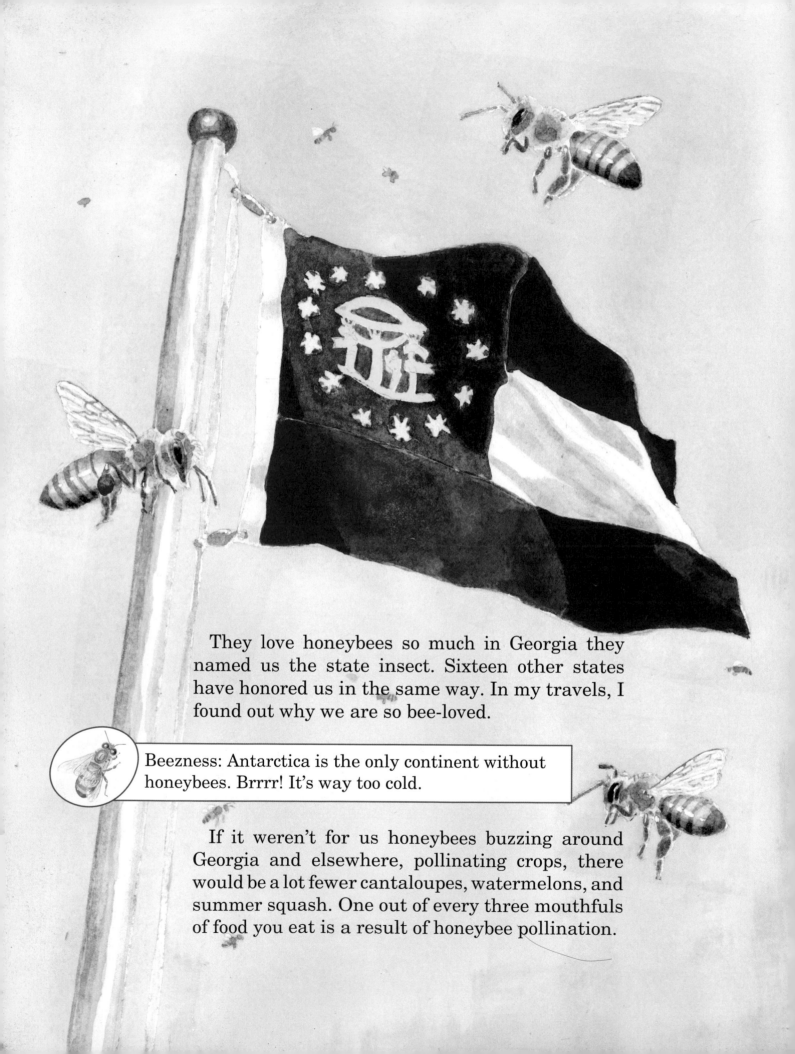

They love honeybees so much in Georgia they named us the state insect. Sixteen other states have honored us in the same way. In my travels, I found out why we are so bee-loved.

Beezness: Antarctica is the only continent without honeybees. Brrrr! It's way too cold.

If it weren't for us honeybees buzzing around Georgia and elsewhere, pollinating crops, there would be a lot fewer cantaloupes, watermelons, and summer squash. One out of every three mouthfuls of food you eat is a result of honeybee pollination.

Pollination is the transfer of pollen from one flower to another to help the plant reproduce. Pollen and nectar from flowers provide food and energy to help us fly back to the hive. When at home, we use the nectar to make honey and the pollen to make bee bread to feed the bee larvae. Nice arrangement, don't you think?

The honey we make is the only food made by insects. It is also the only food that never spoils. You can keep honey forever and it will still taste good. It may crystallize, but if you put the container in a bowl of warm water, the honey will become liquid again.

There are more than three hundred different kinds of honey in the United States. My favorite kind is sourwood honey, which comes from the nectar of the sourwood tree. But don't worry; sourwood honey doesn't turn me from Itty Bitty Betty into Bitter Betty.

Beezness: Honey is 25 percent sweeter than table sugar and is not an empty calorie. It has lots of nutrients. When runners carried the Olympic torch through Hahira, Georgia on their way to the Atlanta Games in 1996, residents handed them honey sticks for instant energy.

I guess I should "back up" here. You know, bees can fly forwards, sideways, and backwards using our two pairs of wings.

We bees live in large groups called *colonies*. Our home is called a *hive*, with three types of bees living there: the *queen*, the *drones*, and the *workers*, like me.

The queen is the largest bee in the colony. There is only one queen per colony. Her job is to make new bees. The drones are the male bees. Their purpose is to mate with the queen.

Worker   Queen   Drone

We worker bees are the smallest bees in the hive. That's why I'm called *Itty Bitty* Betty. We have many jobs. There might be 60,000 of us buzzing around one hive. Some of us might feed bee bread to the larvae or royal jelly to the queen. Some might fan the honey cells to harden the wax that seals them. Some might be the cleanup crew, for we honeybees are very neat and tidy. Some might guard the entrance to the hive. Some might be forager bees, traveling several miles from home to gather pollen and nectar.

My hive has gotten too large, so the buzz is that *we are going to swarm!* Some of us will leave and make a new hive.

Our queen will lead us. Others will stay behind and make a new queen. The queen lets out a certain scent called a *pheromone*. We workers recognize this smell and follow her. We have a better sense of smell than any bloodhound!

Our old queen will find a place to land. It might be a tree trunk or a baseball field or a wing of a plane. Anything's possible.

One time the San Diego Padres were playing the Houston Astros in San Diego. At the bottom of the ninth inning, a swarm of bees appeared. The frightened baseball players swarmed too, running off the field. The game was stopped and an area beekeeper was called.

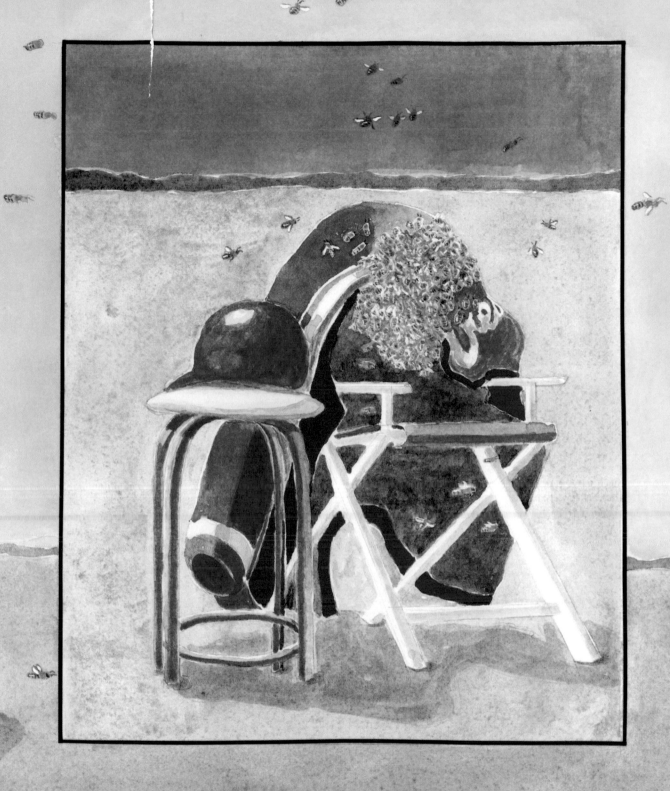

The bees swarmed around a chair that held the
ball girl's jacket. The bees were sprayed to restore
order, and the game resumed.

At Beverly Airport in Beverly, Massachusetts, a swarm of 10,000 honeybees landed on a wing of a parked airplane. A local bee-removal expert was called.

He brought a specially designed bee vacuum cleaner to suck up the bees into a container. He took the bees to an empty hive on his property, where they are still buzzing about their experience.

Jim Ovbey, a beekeeper from Marietta, Georgia, is always on the lookout for bees swarming from his hive. One time, a swarm landed on a tree limb. He cut off the branch and put it on a white sheet. He knocked the limb so that the bees dropped onto the sheet.

Then he separated the marked queen from the swarm and placed her in a new hive. The rest of the bees followed her scent, marching into the new hive in an orderly procession just as if they were going to church.

Beezness: Swarming bees are killed only if they present a public nuisance or a danger.

Old legends say that if bees swarm, we're telling you news of an important event. If we fly into a house, a stranger is coming to visit. If we land on a roof, we bring good luck.

Some people still believe in *tanging the bees*, which causes swarming bees to settle. To coax us into a waiting hive that is coated with honey, someone might beat on a metal pan with a key or spoon to make a tanging or twanging sound. We're happy to go in, because we're hungry!

Tanging might also warn the neighborhood of swarming bees. In olden days, tanging was a way for a beekeeper to make a claim on a swarm of bees and keep other beekeepers away.

Don't get scared if you see us swarming. Although we worker bees have stingers, we sting only when we have no other choice.

After all, we have only one sting in us and are probably more afraid of you than you are of us.

We are swarming tomorrow. There is much to do.
I hope we swarm near a sourwood tree. My mouth is
watering already.

I may be called Itty Bitty Betty, but we honeybees are very important. The next time you enjoy a juicy watermelon or put delicious honey on your biscuit, think of me.

And that's the buzz from me.